Beginning with God
The family guide to the Christian faith

written by Nancy Gorrell
illustrated by Marianne Smith

Christian Focus Publications

Geanies House, Fearn, Tain, Ross-shire, IV20 1TW
Scotland, UK (www.christianfocus.com)

Look out for the next
two books in the series
I Can Know God
by Nancy Gorrell
and illustrated by Marianne Smith.

Meeting with God

Creation   Jesus   Salvation

Living with God

Worship   Heaven   Obedience   Prayer

© 1999 Nancy Gorrell
Published by Christian Focus Publications Ltd
Geanies House, Fearn, Tain, Ross-shire IV20 1TW

Illustrations by Marianne Smith Written by Nancy Gorrell
ISBN 1-85792-453-3

Author's Dedication: This book is dedicated to your covenant children and to mine—Lydia, Austin, and Joshua—my precious sources of inspiration and joy.

Author's Acknowledgment: With thanks to Dr. Morton H. Smith, Dean of Faculty and Systematic Theology professor at Greenville Presbyterian Theological Seminary, for his careful reading and helpful suggestions. And with love and gratitude to my husband, my meticulous proofreader, finest teacher, and closest friend.

This book belongs to our family.
Our names are...

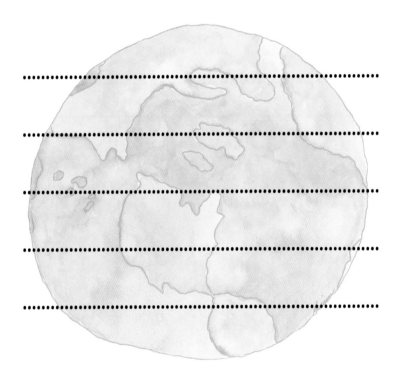

....

....

....

....

....

As for me and my household, we will
serve The Lord. Joshua 24:15

Contents Page

I can know God

Look out for the memory verses at the bottom of each page.
Read and try to remember as many as you can.
Every time you do a memory verse you can tick a box at the end of the book.

God

What is God like? What an excellent question to ask! God is more wonderful than you could ever imagine. He is so amazing and special, so beautiful and great, that you can spend your whole life learning about Him. You can discover something exciting about God every day!

Because God made you, you are precious to Him, and He has many things to teach you about Himself and His world. As you grow older, you may be able to understand more, but there are important truths that you should know now. You are never too little to learn about our wonderful God.

Who among the gods is like you O Lord?... Majestic in holiness, awesome in glory, working wonders
Exodus 15:11

What does God look like? He is very different from you. He is a **Spirit!** That means He is real and living, but that He doesn't have a body — no toes, or fingers, or legs, or hair. You cannot see or touch God.

When the Bible talks about God having arms, it is a picture to help us understand that God is **powerful**, or very strong.

He does not need skinny little arms like yours to do things. He created the world by only speaking words!

**God is spirit and His worshippers must worship in spirit and in truth.
John 4:24**

When the Bible talks about the eyes of God, that is also a picture to help us understand that God **sees**, and **knows, everything.** Even if you hide in the closet (behind the coats!), God can see you, and He knows what you're thinking while you're hiding there, too!

You are familiar with all my ways.
Psalm 139:3

Will God always be here?

God is **_infinite_**. He fills all space. He cannot get lost or locked in a room. Everywhere that you go,

God is with you. God will always be there to help His children when they need Him.

God is **_eternal_**. He was never born, as your baby sister or brother or cousin was. He will never die. You can spend every day of your whole life with God!

But the Lord is the true God; He is the living God, the eternal King.
Jeremiah 10:10

God will **never change.** He doesn't forget about you, or have bad moods like your friends do sometimes.

He won't get busy and ignore you for a while. You can be sure that He will always keep the promises that He makes to you.

I the Lord do not change.
Malachi 3:6

Is God perfect?

God is **holy.** In every way He is high above everything else that exists. He is completely perfect, never doing anything wrong. God calls you to be holy too. But you cannot be perfect! You can be holy by living your life for God.

He is the Rock, His ways are perfect.
Deuteronomy 32:4

God is **good**. Just look at all the good things He gives! The sunshine, the rain, flowers, food, and clothes are just some of His gifts.

Think of all the wonderful things that He has given to you, especially!

Maybe you have a healthy body, or a loving family, or a cosy house, or kind friends. Every good thing that you have is a gift from God.

Every good and perfect gift is from above.
James 1:17

God is **just**. God will never be unfair. He will never dislike you for the size of your feet (or nose or ears) or for the colour of your skin. God can see into your heart! This truth also means that you can never fool God with a lot of money or a nice dress or a pretend smile.

God **never lies**. He won't tease you or trick you. You can open the Book that He wrote for **you** and believe it with your whole heart!

The Lord loves righteousness and justice.
Psalm 33:5

You can learn more about God. Do you know which Book it is that He wrote for you? It is the Bible.

The Bible will tell you more about how wonderful and special, how **glorious,** God is.

It will tell you of the good things God has done for you. God's Book is the most important Book you can ever read. It must make you very happy that God wants even little children like you to know about Him!

I, the Lord, speak the truth.
Isaiah 45:19

The Bible

God in Heaven has written a Book for you. It is the most important Book you will ever read. Does it surprise you that God would write a Book for *you?* Why did He do it?

For the word of the Lord is right and true.
Psalm 33:4

When you go outside at night and see the big sky and the stars, or when you see the beautiful flowers in the daytime, you know that God is very powerful and good. But the flowers don't talk to you and tell you everything that God has done for you.

God wrote a Book so that you would know about Him and His love for His children.

Your word is a lamp to my feet and a light for my path.
Psalm 119:105

In God's Book you learn what is right and wrong. You learn about Jesus and how He died to save grown-ups and little children just like *you!* That is why God wrote His book.

But you are very smart and say, "If God does not have fingers, how can He write a Book?" God used people to write His book.

and God said... 'Write in a book all the words I have spoken to you.'
Jeremiah 30:2

But if people wrote it, how is it God's Book? This is what we call *inspiration*: God worked in the hearts and minds and lives of the special people He chose to write His Book. They wrote it perfectly, just what God wanted them to say, because He helped them.

God's Book is called the *Bible*. It is made up of 66 smaller books in one big Book. It is full of wonderful stories.

The words of the Lord are flawless.
Psalm 12:6

It tells of important things that have already happened and that will happen. It tells us the truth about God, and it teaches us about God's wonderful Son, the Lord Jesus.

Preserve my life, O Lord, according to your love.
All your words are true; all your righteous laws are eternal.
Psalm 119:159-160

Because God wrote this Book, everything in it is true! This is called **inerrancy**. God's Bible has no errors, or mistakes, in it. God does not lie; He does not forget. He does not make things up or say things that are untrue. Everything he says is for our good.

God loves little children and He speaks to them in His Bible in ways that they can understand. Some parts will be harder for you, and you will know more as you grow older. But the most important things for you to know and believe about how to be **saved** have been kept very clear for you.

The Son of God has come and has given us understanding.
1 John 5:20

Even though God's Bible is wonderful, and clear, and beautiful, and good, we do not believe it unless God helps us.

Ask God to teach you His truth every day. So that you can know the important things God tells you in His Bible, learn to read it as soon as you can. Ask grown-ups who know and love God and His Book to help you.

Guide me in your truth and teach me.
Psalm 25:5

You should be glad that God has written a Book so that you can know more and more about Him and His Son, Jesus. And when you love God and believe and obey His Book, be sure to thank Him with your whole heart!

Give thanks to the Lord, call on his name.
Isaiah 12:4

The Trinity

Guess what! You're standing on a big ball! Yes, you are. Did you know that the earth is like a big ball out in space? It's not the only big ball, either. There are many stars and planets and other interesting things in our very, very big universe.

People look up at the sky with special instruments called telescopes, and they can tell many things about space that we can't see with just our eyes.

**The heavens declare the glory of God,
the skies proclaim the work of His hands.
Psalm 19:1**

How do we know that God is good?

God gave man the ability to study and learn about the world He created. Some things about our world are hard to understand. Some people take out their telescopes (for looking at things far away) and microscopes (for looking at things very small).

This helps them learn about God's world.

Everything that man looks at in God's creation shows him that God is wonderful and powerful and wise and good.

The heavens proclaim His righteousness,
and all the peoples see His glory.
Psalm 97:6

But people can't point a telescope up toward heaven and study God. God is a spirit. The Bible tells us that no man has seen God. So how can we find out more about God?

In His Bible God tells us many things about Himself and what He has done. So that is where we must look. Remember too, that we will never be able to understand everything about God because we're not God! Our brains can't fit it all in! Nevertheless, in His Bible God has told us things that we should know and believe.

**Heaven and earth will pass away, but my words will never pass away.
Matthew 24:35**

One of the most important things that we can learn from the Bible is that there is only one God. That means He is the only One that we are to sing to, pray to and worship.

Worship the Lord your God, and serve Him only.
Matthew 4:10

Now I will ask you a tricky question. Did you ever sing a song to Jesus or say a prayer to Him? Why do people in the New Testament worship Jesus? Is Jesus God? Yes. But isn't He God's Son? Yes. Does that make more than one God? No.

This is very hard to understand, isn't it? God is not like you or your mum or your dad. That is why we must go to God's Bible to learn more about Him. Because He is so special, He has to tell us about Himself.

I am the first and I am the last; apart from me there is no God. Who then is like me? Let him proclaim it.
Isaiah 44: 6-7

The Bible tells us that there is one God. The Bible also tells us that this one God **exists** (lives, or is) in three Persons: ***God the Father, God the Son, and God the Holy Spirit.*** They are all one God, but they are all **distinct** Persons (they don't get all mixed up with each other). This is called the ***Trinity,*** and it is a very important truth about God.

The three Persons in the Trinity are all powerful, infinite, eternal, wise, holy, good, just, truthful, and unchanging. No one of the three is more important or more powerful than the others.

Anyone who comes to God must believe that He exists.
Hebrews 11: 6

They have always been Father, Son, and Holy Spirit, and they never trade names or change places.

The Bible tells us that each Person of the Trinity does all the things that God does and that they each have special work. God the Father sent God the Son to become a man, to die for His children, and to earn their salvation. God the Father and God the Son send God the Holy Spirit to change the hearts of God's people and to cause them to love and obey God.

For God so loved the world that He gave His one and only Son, that whoever believes in Him shall not perish but have eternal life.
John 3:16

Can I understand everything about God?

The **doctrine** (teaching) of the Trinity is one of the most difficult facts in the Bible. Many people refuse to believe this truth because they cannot fully understand it. (They forget that they are not God and that He is too big to fit into their little minds.)

Other people pretend that they believe the Bible, but they make up amazing and terrible stories about God or Jesus or the Holy Spirit, to make them more like people, so that they can understand.

Let the wicked forsake his way and the evil man his thoughts. Let him turn to the Lord, and He will have mercy on him.
Isaiah 55:7

Does thinking about "God is one and God exists in three Persons" give you a headache? Does it make you tired or confused or upset?

Don't be! You should be glad, oh so glad, that you cannot understand everything about God. No person can do that — not you, your mum, your dad, your pastor, anyone.

If they could, He wouldn't be God! God is perfect; God is big; God is very, very different from us.

**'For my thoughts are not your thoughts,
neither are your ways my ways,' declares the Lord.
Isaiah 55:8**

Do you love God for how special He is? Are you thankful for the truths that He tells you about Himself, even if they are hard to understand? Do you believe these things that God teaches you in His Bible?

If you say no to these questions, ask God — Father, Son, and Holy Spirit — to change your heart and forgive you for not believing Him. If you can say yes, you should stop right now and thank God — Father, Son, and Holy Spirit — for the special gift of faith that He has given you.

Help me overcome my unbelief.
Mark 9:24

MEMORY VERSES:

Get someone to test you to see how many verses you can remember!
Tick a box when you have learnt a verse.

Who among the gods is like you O Lord?... Majestic in holiness,
awesome in glory working wonders. Exodus 15:11

God is spirit and His worshippers must worship in spirit and in truth.
John 4:24

You are familiar with all my ways. Psalm 139:3

But the Lord is the true God; He is the living God, the eternal King.
Jeremiah 10:10

I the Lord do not change. Malachi 3:6

He is the Rock, His ways are perfect. Deuteronomy 32:4

Every good and perfect gift is from above. James 1:17

The Lord loves righteousness and justice. Psalm 33:5

I, the Lord, speak the truth. Isaiah 45:19

MEMORY VERSES:

For the word of the Lord is right and true.
Psalm 33:4

Your word is a lamp to my feet and a light for my path.
Psalm 119:105

and God said... 'Write in a book all the words I have
spoken to you.' Jeremiah 30:2

The words of the Lord are flawless.
Psalm 12:6

Preserve my life, O Lord, according to your love.
All your words are true; all your righteous laws are eternal.
Psalm 119:159-160

The Son of God has come and given us understanding.
1 John 5:20

Guide me in your truth and teach me. Psalm 25:5

Give thanks to the Lord, call on His name.
Isaiah 12:4

MEMORY VERSES:

The heavens declare the glory of God, the skies proclaim the work of His hands. Psalm 19:1

The heavens proclaim His righteousness, and all the peoples see His glory. Psalm 97:6

Heaven and earth will pass away but my words will never pass away. Matthew 24:35

Worship the Lord your God, and serve Him only. Matthew 4:10

I am the first and I am the last; apart from me there is no God. Who then is like me? Let him proclaim it. Isaiah 44: 6-7

Anyone who comes to God must believe that He exists. Hebrews 11:6

God so loved the world that He gave His one and only Son, that whoever believes in Him shall not perish but have eternal life. John 3:16

Let the wicked forsake his way and the evil man his thoughts. Let him turn to the Lord, and He will have mercy on him. Isaiah 55:7

'For my thoughts are not your thoughts, neither are your ways my ways,' declares the Lord. Isaiah 55:8

Help me overcome my unbelief.
Mark 9:24